THE UK SLOW COOKER RECIPE BOOK

Tasty and Nutritious Recipes for The Whole Family incl. Vegetarian Bonus

SARAH L. TAYLOR

ISBN - 9798654233813

TABLE OF CONTENTS

INTRODUCTION

Throw everything in one pot, head out to work, and come home to a meal ready to eat? Through the use of a slow cooker, this is completely possible. Though it may not be as trendy as other kitchen gadgets, sometimes going back to the simpler days is exactly what a family needs. In fact, many of the meals that are cooked in this amazing kitchen appliancecan be delicious and even healthy.

Slow Cooker – What is it?

The slow cooker has found a home in kitchens across the globe for decades. This appliance makes making dinner easy, and with the world becoming more and more hectic, that is nice. The design of the units is very simple. The cooker comes with a heating component and an earthenware interior compartment used to house the ingredients of the delicious meal you are looking to whip up.

How Does It Work?

The cooking process of a slow cooker is much like that of a Dutch oven. You place the Dutch oven on the stove, and the heat of the stove builds up upwards into the dish . The heat retained by the dish is then dispersed into the food within. A slow cooker works similarly, as we have said. The heating element that is built into the bottom of the housing heats the earthenware insert With a sealed lid, the heat and moisture are kept in the unit. This cooks your food slowly and is perfect for tender meat and vegetables alike.

Maintenance

There is not a lot of maintenance required when dealing with a slow cooker. Of the possible maintenance needed perhaps this most important is keeping your unit clean. By doing this, you will extend its life and ensure that your meals are perfectly cooked. The first step is to ensure that the unit is unplugged and if it has been used recently, cooled off completely. The lid and insert are simple to clean as it is done the old fashioned way with soap and water in the sink. If, however you choose to clean it the old school way there are a few things tips that will help you:

- Stay away from abrasive cleaners and tools. You should use a standard sponge. If there are stuck on bits, scrape them off with a plastic spatula.

- Vinegar can work wonders. It can be used to get rid of dirt and grime.

- Use hot water to clean your insert; cold water will just not get the job done.

- Never submerge the base that houses the heating element in water. Instead, wait until the unit is cooled down and take a damp washcloth to it. Then take a rag and dry thoroughly before storing.

You will also want to ensure all the components are in peak condition. That means if something starts to act up, it is probably best to look for a replacement part. If you can't find one, it might be time to get a new unit.

Tips and Tricks

Even though this device is simple to use and maintain, there are still some tips and tricks that may help you elevate your meal preparation.

Not All Meat is Designed For the Slow Cooker

The slow cooker is designed to cook meals over long periods, and that means that some of the more choice cuts will not work well in it. You should look for cuts that are tougher or even larger like roasts. The great thing is that a slow cooker is pretty fool-proof, and that means tender meat every time as long as you pick the right cut.

Brown Your Meat Before

Sure it would be easier just to throw everything in the pot and leave it to cook. Butif delicious well-cooked meats are what you are after then adding this extra step is in order. You should brown most meats before placing them in the slow cooker. This will enhance the final look and improve the overall flavor of the meat too. On top of that, you can deglaze the skillet and get even more flavor.

Quality Over Quantity

Making sure to read the manual is key. Each slow cooker will have rules for the fill level for optimal results. For the most part, the best rule to live by is to not fill the cooker over two thirds full. If you put too much in the insert, the unit may not come up to proper temperature which couldlead to food safety concerns and affect the overall cooking times. Plus, the process of cooking using this methodcreates more liquids, and the unit doesn't allow much evaporation. This could lead to overflow.

Thaw First, Cook Second

Small volume things like peas and corn can be cooked from frozen, but for the most part, it is best to thaw everything out prior to cooking.

Dairy Is Last In Line

If you are preparing a recipe that contains any dairy, then you will want to add it in at the right time. This means that it should go in last.

Most dairy will break down and potentially separate when cooked too long. This is why it is better to add it in the end.

Safety First

Though a slow cooker can run all day long or even overnight, you should stay safe and follow the safety guidelines laid out in the manual.

- Some other fun tips:
  - » Use non-stick cooking spray to coat the insert . This will help the clean up process move along quicker
  - » Also, invest in liner bags made for slow cookers. Using these will also make cleaning up quicker.
  - » High settings for most slow cookers are about 138°C. While the low tends to hover around 77°C.
  - » The cooking ratio is one hour on high equals two hours on low.
  - » Adding fresh herbs towards the end will helpliven up the flavors.
  - » Heartier vegetables like potatoes should go in the pot first. This will allow them to cook properly..

RECIPES

BREAKFAST

SAUSAGE & VEGETABLE BREAKFAST CASSEROLE

Servings: 9

INGREDIENTS

- 12 lrg. eggs
- 118 ml milk
- ½ tsp. garlic salt
- 1 tsp. salt
- ½ pkg. hash browns
- 2 pkgs. chicken sausage
- 2 bell peppers, red, diced
- 1 bell pepper, green, diced
- ½ onion, diced fine
- 60g spinach, baby, chopped
- 113g cheddar, shredded
- 2 tbsps. parsley, fresh, chopped

DIRECTIONS

1. Mix the eggs, milk, salt, and garlic salt together in a mixing bowl. Prepare the vegetables and sausage.

2. Spray the insert of the slow cooker with nonstick cooking spray. Add in everything but the egg mixture and cheese; mix together.

3. Then top with egg mixture evenly. Top the ingredienst with cheese and then cover. On low cook the casserole 6-8 hours or until eggs have set. Serve garnished with parsley.

Nutritional Facts:

Calories: 170

Proteins: 13g

Carbs: 5g

Fats: 11g

HOLIDAY INSPIRED OATMEAL

Servings: 4

INGREDIENTS

- ◆ 312g oats, steel-cut
- ◆ .95L eggnog
- ◆ .95L water
- ◆ 100g cranberries, fresh

DIRECTIONS

1. Add all the ingredients into the insert of the slow cooker.

2. Set the cooker to low and let cook for approximately 4 hours. Serve warm garnished with a little cinnamon and nutmeg.

Nutritional Facts:
Calories: 540
Proteins: 26g
Carbs: 75g
Fats: 16g

BREAKFAST BURRITO

Servings: 8

INGREDIENTS

- 425g black beans
- 1 pkg. tofu, crumbles
- 25g scallions, chopped
- 1 bell pepper, green, chopped fine
- 256g salsa
- 118 mL water
- ½ tsp. ground turmeric
- ¼ tsp. ground cumin
- ¼ tsp. chili powder
- ½ tsp. smoked paprika
- salt & pepper to taste
- 90g spinach, fresh, chopped
- 8 whole-wheat tortillas
- Avocado
- Cheddar, shredded
- Salsa

DIRECTIONS

1. Place beans, tofu, scallions, bell pepper, salsa, salt, pepper, water, turmeric, cumin, chili powder, and paprika into the slow cooker in the cooker. Turn cooker onto the low setting and let cook for about 6 hours..

2. After the six hours are up you can add in the spinach and let it heat up.

3. Take a spoon with slots and spoon the mixture into the tortilla. Add your favorite burrito toppings and then roll the burrito.

4. Top with additional salsa, hot sauce, or whatever else you like.

Nutritional Facts:

Calories: 170

Proteins: 8g

Carbs: 27g

Fats: 4.5g

15

AUTUMNAL BAKED APPLE

Servings: 8

INGREDIENTS

- 4 apples
- Cherry juice (to your taste)
- Dried cherries
- 61g granola
- 1 tsp. cinnamon
- 1 tbsp. butter

DIRECTIONS

1. Cut off the tops of the apples and hollow the center out. Place dried cherries in water and let them rehydrate. Mix the granola an cinnamon and then add the juice to the mixture. Add the cherries and mix well cherries in.

2. Fill every apple with the granola blend. Top every apple with a little pat of butter.

3. Place applis into the cooker and set on low for 4 hours.

4. Serve topped with Greek yogurt and some additional granola.

Nutritional Facts:

Calories: 100

Proteins: 1g

Carbs: 17g

Fats: 3.5g

SLOW COOKER BREAKFAST POTATOES

Servings: 8

INGREDIENTS

- ◆ 1.36kg baby potatoes, diced
- ◆ 1 bell pepper, green, diced
- ◆ 1 bell pepper, red, diced
- ◆ ½ onion, diced fine
- ◆ 3 cloves garlic, minced
- ◆ 2 tsps. salt
- ◆ 2 tsps. smoked paprika
- ◆ 2 tbsps. butter
- ◆ 2 tbsps. olive oil, extra virgin
- ◆ Salt & pepper to taste

DIRECTIONS

1. Using a nonstick cooking spray lightly coat the cookers insert. Add in the potatoes, bell peppers, onion, garlic, salt, paprika, and butter. Sprinkle the olive oil on top of the mixture and mix together.

2. Spread evenly, then set the temperature to low and let cook for 4-5 hours. .

3. Mix well and then season to taste with salt and pepper.

Nutritional Facts:

Calories: 190

Proteins: 4g

Carbs: 32g

Fats: 6g

BANANA – CHOCOLATE CHIP BREAKFAST BAR

Servings: 6

INGREDIENTS

- 3 bananas
- 237 mL fruit purée
- ½ tsp. vanilla extract
- 80g almond milk
- 125g whole wheat flour
- 156g oats
- 2 tsps. baking powder
- ½ tsp. salt
- 85g chocolate chips, dark
- 30g powdered sugar
- 1 tbsp. cinnamon
- 1 tsp. milk

DIRECTIONS

1. Place ripe banans into bowl and mash them until smooth. Add the fruit purée, vanilla, and almond milk into a bowl. Mix until combined.

2. In the same bowl add the flour, oats, baking powder, and salt. Mix until blended thoroughly.

3. With cooking spray lightly coat the slow cooker. Then line the insert with parchment paper.

4. Empty batter into cooker and top with chocolate chips. Spread evenly and cook on low until the edges are lightly browned (about 2 hours), and a toothpick can be inserted and removed clean.

5. Turn the cooker off and let cool. When it's cool, lift the bars, using the parchment paper, out of the cooker. Place on a cooling rack.

6. While the bars are cooling down, put the cinaamon drizzle together. Combine the powdered sugar, cinnamon, and milk. When the bars have cooled, drizzle the cinnamon mixture over the top and serve.

Nutritional Facts:

Calories: 390

Proteins: 7g

Carbs: 70g

Fats: 10g

SPINACH & CHEESE FRITTATA

Servings: 6

INGREDIENTS

- 1 tbsp. olive oil, extra-virgin
- 80g onion, diced
- 112g mozzarella, shredded
- 3 eggs
- 3 egg whites
- 2 tbsps. milk
- ¼ tsp. pepper
- ¼ tsp white pepper
- 1 pkg. baby spinach, thawed pressed and chopped
- 1 tomato, diced
- salt to taste

DIRECTIONS

1. Heat oil in a skillet over medium heat. Then add the onions and saute them until softened.

2. Lightly coat the cooker wth a cooking spray. Combine the onions as well as the rest of the ingredients (excluding a quarter of the cheese).. Once the egg mixture is poured into the slow cooker top with the cheese your set aside.

3. Evenly spread this mixture out and for half an hour cook on low until the eggs are set.

Nutritional Facts:

Calories: 140

Proteins: 10g

Carbs: 4g

Fats: 9g

MEXICAN CASSEROLE

Servings: 4

INGREDIENTS

- 1 tsp. olive oil
- 225g potatoes, diced small
- 128g salsa
- 40g onion, diced
- 1 jalapeño, diced
- 5 lrg. eggs
- 56g mozzarella, shredded
- ¼ tsp. salt
- 1/8 tsp. pepper

DIRECTIONS

1. Rub olive oil on all sides of the cooker. Add in the potatoes, onions, jalapeno, and salsa inside the cooker.

2. In a large mixing bowl, whisk the eggs. Toss in the mozzarella, salt, and pepper. Mix this and pour it into the slow cooker.

3. Set the cooker on low and cook for 4 hours.

Nutritional Facts:
Calories: 190
Proteins: 13g
Carbs: 13g
Fats: 10g

PUMPKIN FRENCH TOAST

Servings: 4

INGREDIENTS

- 245g pumpkin puree
- 0.83L milk
- 73g coconut sugar
- 3 eggs
- 2 tsps. pumpkin pie seasoning
- 2 tsps. cinnamon
- 2 tsps. vanilla extract
- ¼ tsp. salt
- 340g whole wheat bread, cut into cubes
- Cooking spray

DIRECTIONS

1. Blend the pumpkin, milk, coconut sugar, eggs, and seasonings in a bowl. Whisk together until smooth.

2. Add the bread in the bowl and coat all the pieces. Spread evenly and let set in the refrigerator until the custard is soaked into the bread.

3. Coat the slow cooker lightly with cooking spray. Pour French toast into the cooker and evenly spread it out.

4. Cook on low for 7-8 hours. Serve topped with spiced whipped cream or yogurt.

Nutritional Facts:

Calories: 530
Proteins: 25g
Carbs: 79g
Fats: 12g

CINNAMON ROLLS

Servings: 12

INGREDIENTS

- 177 ml milk
- ½ tbsp. butter, melted
- 2 tbsps. coconut sugar
- ½ tsp. salt
- 2¼ tsps. dry yeast
- 300g whole wheat flour
- 6 tbsps. coconut sugar
- 2 tsps. ground cinnamon
- ½ tbsp. butter, melted

DIRECTIONS

1. Line the slow cooker with aluminum foil and coat the foil with non-stick cooking splash. Wipe up extra, so there are no pools of spray.

2. In a mixing bowl, combine the milk, butter, sugar, and salt. Sprinkle the yeast on top. Let sit until the blend foams. Then add 1 ½ cups of flour. Add flour until you can see the batter begin to form a ball.

3. Pour the mixture onto a floured working surface. Knead the dough until it becomes springy. Then let it rest.

4. While it is setting, make the filling. Add the sugar and cinnamon into a mixing bowl.

5. On a floured surface, turn the dough out into a 16x10" square shape. Brush with the melted butter, leaving a 1" edge on the longer sides. Sprinkle with the cinnamon sugar, leaving a 1" border on the longer sides as well. Carefully begin to roll the dough into alog. Squeeze the end of the dough to seal.

6. Cut the log into 12 pieces utilizing a sharp serrated blade. Spot the folds into the prepared cooker and place the lid on top. Turn the cooker to its "Keep Warm" setting and let rise for 30-45 minutes.

7. Without removing the cover, turn the cooker to its low. Cook rolls until the filling isbubbling which should be about an hour and a half. Cool for approximately 10 minutes before lifting the foil out of the cooker and serving.

Nutritional Facts:

Calories: 130
Proteins: 4g
Carbs: 26g
Fats: 1.5g

GREEK BREAKFAST CASSEROLE

Servings: 7

INGREDIENTS

- 12 large eggs
- 177ml almond milk
- ½ tsp. salt
- ½ tsp. pepper
- ½ tsp. garlic powder
- ¼ tsp. onion powder
- 0.71L bread, dried, cubed
- 227g spinach, frozen, defrosted and squeezed
- 75g feta, crumbled
- 27g sun-dried tomatoes, sliced

DIRECTIONS

1. Oil the cooker with non-stick oil spray.

2. Add the eggs to a bowl and whisk together. Include the milk, garlic powder,onion power, salt and pepper. Then mix to combine. Set to the side.

3. Place the bread in the cooker in an even layer. Sprinkle the spinach, feta, and sun-dried tomatoes over the top evenly.

4. Pour the eggs evenly over the mixture. Cook on low for around 3 hours.

Nutritional Facts:
Calories: 180
Proteins: 15g
Carbs: 6g
Fats: 12g

HUEVOS RANCHEROS

Servings: 6

INGREDIENTS

- 1 tbsp. olive oil
- 1 onion, diced
- 1 bell pepper, red
- 1 jalapeno
- 3 cloves garlic, diced fine
- 480g canned tomatoes, diced
- 1 tbsp. cumin seeds
- 425g black beans
- 6 large eggs
- ¼ tsp. chili powder
- 6 corn tortillas
- 1 avocado
- 38g feta, crumbled
- 2 tbsps. cilantro, fresh, chopped
- 2 tsps. lime juice, fresh

DIRECTIONS

1. Over medium high heat warm the oil in a large skillet. Add the onion, bell pepper, and jalapeño, and sauté until One the oil is warmed toss in the onion, jalepeno, and pepper. Cook until lightly browned , around 8 minutes. Then include garlic and sauté until fragrant, approximately 30 seconds.

2. In the meantime, spray the slow cooker with cooking spray. Mix tomatoes and juices, cumin seeds, and chile powder together in a bowl. Fill the cooker, using a third of the mixture. Take half of the pepper/onion mix and add it on top of that. .

3. Repeat the process until both mixtures are all in the slow cooker. Set the cooker on low and cook for about 8-9 hours. In the morning, cook the eggs, seasoned with salt and pepper, in batches.

4. To serve, top every tortilla with ¾ cup tomato blend and 1 egg. Top with avocado, feta, cilantro, and lime juice. Serve warm topped with sour cream and garnished with a little cilantro.

Nutritional Facts:
Calories: 320
Proteins: 16g
Carbs: 34g
Fats: 15g

PORTOBELLO EGG CUPS

Servings: 8

INGREDIENTS

- 4 eggs
- 2 portobello mushroom tops
- 0.79kg canned tomatoes, crushed
- 1 bell pepper, chopped
- 1 onion, chopped
- 1 clove garlic, minced
- 1 tsp. paprika
- 1 tsp. salt
- ½ tsp. pepper
- ½ tsp. thyme

DIRECTIONS

1. Combine the tomatoes, bell pepper, onion, garlic, paprika, salt, pepper, and thyme to the slow cooker. Mix well.

2. Clean the mushroom tops with a damp paper towel. Make sure to clean out the gills and get rid of the stems.. Then set the cleaned mushrooms in the cooker with the cup portion up. Sprinkle salt and pepper on top.

3. Cook on low for 4-6 hours.

4. Split egg(s) into each mushroom top. Season with salt and pepper. Cook an extra 5-10 minutes on HIGH or until eggs are cooked to your liking.

Nutritional Facts:
Calories: 80
Proteins: 6g
Carbs: 9g
Fats: 2.5g

EGGS ON CAULIFLOWER HASH

Servings: 4

INGREDIENTS

- ♦ 454g riced cauliflower
- ♦ 2 eggs
- ♦ 1 egg white
- ♦ ¼ tsp. garlic powder
- ♦ ½ tsp. salt
- ♦ ½ tsp. pepper
- ♦ 57g cheddar, shredded
- ♦ 1 scallion, chopped
- ♦ 30g white whole wheat flour
- ♦ 4 eggs
- ♦ salt
- ♦ pepper

DIRECTIONS

1. Add cauliflower rice toi a good sizedglass bowl and microwave for 3 minutes.

2. Use paper towels to remove any extra water.

3. In a large bowl, mix the riced cauliflower with the remaining ingredienst, excluding the eggs. Then mix until combined.

4. Spray the slow cooker with non-stick cooking spray. Add the cauliflower blend and evenly spread it out. Set the cooker to high and let mix cook for a little over an hour or ntil cauliflower has ligtly brown edges.

5. Then top the cauliflower with the four eggs. Continue cooking for extra 20-30 minutes until eggs are cooked to your prefernce. Then season to taste.

6. Serve with Sriracha, harissa, tzatziki, or pesto.

Nutritional Facts:
Calories: 230
Proteins: 18g
Carbs: 14g
Fats: 12g

LUNCH

SLOPPY JOES GREEK STYLE

Servings: 8

INGREDIENTS

- 454g turkey, ground
- 171g onion, diced
- 3 cloves garlic, minced
- ½ tsp. salt
- ¼ tsp. pepper
- 1 bell pepper, red, chopped

- 1 can chickpeas, rinsed, dried
- 1 can tomato puree
- 2 tbsps. tomato paste
- 1 tbsp. honey
- ½ tsp. dried oregano
- ¼ tsp. ground nutmeg

DIRECTIONS

1. Coat the slow cooker with cooking spray. Over medium high heat in a skillet earm some oil. Add the turkey and onion. Break the turkey up and cook for about six minutes. Then add season with salt and pepper and add the garlic as well. Cook until you begin to smell the garlic. Move the meat ond onions to the cooker.

2. Once that is done include bell pepper, chickpeas, tomato sauce, tomato paste, honey, oregano, and nutmeg. Mix until combined. Cook on low for 4 hours.

3. Then serve spooned onto a whole wheat bun and toppings of your choice.

Nutritional Facts:
Calories: 329
Proteins: 23g
Carbs: 43g
Fats: 9g

CREAMY TOMATO SOUP

Servings: 4

INGREDIENTS

- 1 tbsp. olive oil, extra-virgin
- 512g onions, chopped
- 3 cloves garlic, minced
- 1 can whole tomatoes with juices
- 710ml chicken broth
- 2 tsps. salt
- 1 tsp. hot Hungarian paprika
- ½ tsp. pepper
- 48g whole wheat orzo
- 250ml cream

DIRECTIONS

1. Over medium low heat warm oil. When warmed toss in the onions and cook until lightly brown. At this point add in the garlic and cook until you begin to smell it.

2. Lightly coat the slow cooker with non-stick cooking spray. Add in everything excluding the pasta and cream. Stir until combined. Cook on low for 5 to 6 hours until the tomatoes are extremely delicate. Then in batches, add the soup to a food processor or blender and pulse until smooth. Return pureed soup to the cooker and include the pasta. orzo. Turn cooker to high and let cook until pasta is al dente.

3. Once the pasta is cooked, add the cream , whick to and stir until combine. Top with basil and Parmesan and serve.

Nutritional Facts:

Calories: 176
Proteins: 5g
Carbs: 26g
Fats: 5g

BAKED POTATOES

Servings: 4

INGREDIENTS

- 4 potatoes
- 2 tsps. olive oil
- ½ tsp. salt

DIRECTIONS

1. Clean the potatoes and dry thoroughly. For every potato, using the aluminum foil make little bowls for them in the slow cooker. Prick each potato and set in te fil bowls. Drizzle each potato with ½ teaspoon of olive oil and ¼ tsp. salt. Rub the salt and oil over the outside of the potato, then wrap firmly in the foil. Place in the cooker.

2. Cook the potatoes on low for 8 to 10 hours, until delicate. Then remove from the cooker and the foil. Choose your favorite toppings and then serve.

Nutritional Facts:

Calories: 177

Proteins: 6g

Carbs: 36g

Fats: 2g

TERIYAKI CHICKEN

Servings: 4

INGREDIENTS

- ◆ 226g chicken thighs, boneless, skinless
- ◆ 156ml soy sauce
- ◆ 3 tbsps. rice vinegar
- ◆ 3 tbsps. honey
- ◆ 3 tbsps. brown sugar
- ◆ 1 clove garlic, minced
- ◆ 1 tbsp. ginger, fresh, minced
- ◆ 2 tbsps. water
- ◆ 1 tbsp. cornstarch
- ◆ Toasted sesame seeds
- ◆ Chopped green onions

DIRECTIONS

1. In the cooker lay the chicken in an even layer. .

2. In a medium-sized mixing bowl, whisk together the soy sauce, honey, sugar, rice vinegar garlic, and ginger. Ladle the mixture onto the chicken.

3. Cook on low until the chicken is tender, about for 4 hours. delicate and cooked through. Remove thighs and shred. Strain the cooking fluid into a pan.

4. Add the cornstarch and water into a small bowl and combine until smooth. Add to the pan whith the cooking fluid, whisk to combine. Heat sauce until it reaches a boil. Stir continulsy while it simmers. You can stop when the sauce is thickened then take off of the heat.

5. Add the chicken back into the sauce. Stir until coated. Serve warm with rice garnished with sesame seeds and green onions.

Nutritional Facts:

Calories: 319
Proteins: 35g
Carbs: 28g
Fats: 7g

CHICKEN MEATBALLS W/ BUFFALO SAUCE

Servings: 23 meatballs

INGREDIENTS

- 454g ground chicken
- 80g whole wheat Panko bread crumbs
- 1 lrg. egg
- 1 tsp. salt
- ¾ tsp. garlic powder
- ¼ tsp. pepper
- 2 scallions, chopped fine
- 177ml hot sauce
- Blue cheese, crumbled

DIRECTIONS

1. Preheat the stove to 200°C. Prepare a baking sheet by lining it withaluminum foil and lightly spray it with cooking spray. Uisng the same spray lightly coat the cooker isert too.

2. In a large mixing bowl, place the ground chicken, bread crumbs, egg, salt, garlic powder, pepper, and green onion. Mix the meat and other ingredients together until blended. Shape into 1cm meatballs and place them on the baking sheet.

3. Bake until the meatballs are light brown, then flip them over, cook for about two minutes more.

4. Move the meatballs to the slow cooker. Pour the hot sauce over the meatballs and gently mix to coat. Cook on low for 2 hours.

5. Sprinkle green onions and blue cheese over the meatalls and serve hot.

Nutritional Facts:

Calories: 47

Proteins: 4g

Carbs: 3g

Fats: 2g

HAWAIIAN CHICKEN

Servings: 6

INGREDIENTS

- 907g chicken breasts, boneless, skinless, cubed
- 1 can pineapple chunks in juice
- 2 tbsps. cornstarch
- 59ml soy sauce
- 2 tbsps. garlic, minced
- 1 tbsp. ginger, fresh, minced
- 2 tsps. sesame oil
- ½ tsp. red pepper flakes
- ¼ tsp. pepper
- 2 bell peppers, red, diced
- 1 can water chestnuts
- 2 scallions, chopped

DIRECTIONS

1. Lightly spray a slow cooker with nonstick cooking soray and then lay the chocken in the base Drain the juice form the pineapple into a mixing bowl. Slowly stir in cornstarch. When smooth, add the sesame oil, soy sauce, red pepper flakes, ginger, garlic, and pepper. Mix until combined. Pour over the chicken. Then add in the pineapple chunks and peppers. Set cooker to low and cook for 4-5 hours.

2. Take chcken and veggies out of slow cooker using a slotted spoon and set on a plate. Using a mesh colander strain the cooking fluid into a little pan.Simmer over high until it reduces Let simmer over medium heat until the sauce thickens. Transfer the sauce into the cooker and stir to combine. Now include the scallions and water chestnuts. Mix to combine. Serve over your grain of choice.

Nutritional Facts:
Calories: 383
Proteins: 20g
Carbs: 38g
Fats: 5g

CHICKEN CURRY

Servings: 4

INGREDIENTS

- ◆ 1 lrg. yam, peeled, diced
- ◆ 2 bell peppers, red, diced fine
- ◆ 59ml water
- ◆ 49ml lime juice, fresh
- ◆ 2 tbsps. curry powder
- ◆ 2 tsps. smoked paprika
- ◆ 1 tsp. cumin, ground
- ◆ 1 tsp. chili powder
- ◆ 1 tsp. salt
- ◆ 227g chicken thighs, boneless, skinless
- ◆ 1 tbsp.olive oil, extra virgin
- ◆ 1 can coconut milk
- ◆ 2 tbsps. cornstarch

DIRECTIONS

1. Place the yam and peppers in the slow cooker. Pour the water and lime juice over the top.

2. Add the curry, cumin, chili powder, smoked paprika, , and salt to a small bowl. Place the chicken on a cutting board and sprinkle the two sides with 2/3 of the seasoning mixture. Rub to coat and place the remaining seasoning blend to the side.

3. Heat oil in a skillet over medium-high. When hot, add the chicken thighs and brown on both sides. Then transfer slow cooker, set on the vegetables. Then sprinkle remaining seasonings over the top. Turn cooker on to low and cook for 4 -5 hours.

4. Take chicken out of cooker. Let cool and then shred it with two forks. Set to the side.

5. Pour the coconut milk and cornstarch slurry into the cooker and mix with the vegetables and cooking fluid. Turn the cooker to high and let cook until l the sauce thickens.

6. Return the chicken to the cooker and coat the chicken in the sauce. Let cook together for 15 extra minutes. Serve warm over rice or with naan, finished off with fresh, chopped cilantro.

Nutritional Facts:
Calories: 398
Proteins: 35g
Carbs: 22g
Fats: 18g

BEEF & BROCCOLI

Servings: 4

INGREDIENTS

- 227g flank steak, sliced
- 237ml beef stock
- 59ml soy sauce
- 59ml clam sauce
- 1 tbsp. honey
- 1 tbsp. rice vinegar
- 2 tsps. Sriracha
- 2 tsps. garlic, minced
- 2 tbsps. cornstarch
- 2 sm. heads broccoli, cut

DIRECTIONS

1. Coat the slow cooker with non-stick cooking spray. Place the steak in the base.

2. Add the stock, rice vinegar, clam sauce, soy sauce, garlic, honey, and Sriracha ito a bowl and mix together. Pour mixture over the meat. Cook on low for 1-2 hours.

3. To In a bowl, whisk together 59ml water add cornstarch and whisk to combine. Mix into the cooker and place the broccoli on top. Turn the cooker up to high, and cook for an additional half hour or until the broccoli is tender. Serve warm over rice, sprinkled with green onions and sesame seeds.

Nutritional Facts:

Calories: 519
Proteins: 43g
Carbs: 46g
Fats: 14g

CHEDDAR POTATO SOUP

Servings: 4

INGREDIENTS

- 2 tbsps. butter
- 1 onion, diced
- 3 lrg. carrots, diced
- 907g potatoes, peeled, diced
- 1 tsp. Italian seasoning
- 1 tsp. salt
- ¼ tsp. cayenne pepper
- 710ml chicken stock
- 1 can evaporated milk
- 3 tbsps. cornstarch
- 88g sharp cheddar, shredded
- 237ml plain Greek yogurt

DIRECTIONS

1. Lightly coat the slow cooker with non-stick cooking spray. In a large skillet, melt the butter over medium heat. Then add in the onion and sauté until tender. Add to the cooker.

2. Throw in the carrots, potatoes, Italian seasoning, salt, cayenne, and chicken stock. Stir to combine. Set cooker to low and let cook for 6 -8 hours.

3. While the vegetables cook, combine the ievaporated milk and cornstarch whisking until smooth. During the last 30 minutes of cooking, include the slurry into the cooker. Keep cooking for an additional half hour.

4. Before serving, mix in the cheese and yogurt. With a potato masher, mash half of the potatoes in the slow cooker. Stir to combine and then season to taste.

5. Serve hot topped with bacon, chives, extra cheese and/or yogurt.

Nutritional Facts:

Calories: 418
Proteins: 21g
Carbs: 81g
Fats: 9g

STUFFED BELL PEPPERS

Servings: 6

INGREDIENTS

- 6 bell peppers
- 453g ground chicken
- 1 can black beans, rinsed, drained
- 1 can diced tomatoes with juices
- 565g cauliflower rice
- 2 tsps. chili powder
- 1 tsp. cumin
- 1 tsp. garlic powder
- ½ tsp. salt
- 22g pepper jack cheese, shredded

DIRECTIONS

1. Cut the tops off of the peppers and clean out the insides. Set to the side.

2. Add the chicken to a bowl. In the same bowl add the beans, tomatoes with juices, garlic powder, chili powder, riced cauliflower, cumin, salt, as well as the cheddar. Mix until combined.

3. Spoon the mixture into the emptied-out peppers, filling them to the top.

4. Pour 118ml of water into a slow cooker. Set the peppers sut side up in the water evenly spaced. Set cooker temperature to low and cook for about 6 hours. Remove the top, sprinkle the peppers with extra cheese. Cover the cooker again. Keep covered until the cheddar is melted. Serve hot with favorite garnishes.

Nutritional Facts:
Calories: 355
Proteins: 27g
Carbs: 30g
Fats: 15g

BUTTERNUT SQUASH SOUP

Servings: 8

INGREDIENTS

- ◆ 1 tbsp. olive oil, extra-virgin
- ◆ 1 onion, diced
- ◆ 2 med. butternut squash
- ◆ 2 apples, cored, diced
- ◆ 473ml vegetable stock
- ◆ 1 tsp. salt
- ◆ ½ tsp. ground nutmeg
- ◆ ¼ tsp. pepper
- ◆ ¼ tsp. cayenne pepper
- ◆ 177ml coconut milk

DIRECTIONS

1. Gently coat the slow cooker with non-stick spray. In a medium pot, over medium heat warm the olive oil. Once warm add the onion into skillet. Cook until softened and then move to slow cooker.

2. While the onion cooks, trim the top and base off of the butternut squash. With a vegetable peeler, peel the squash. Cut it down the middle the long way and scoop out the inside seeds. Cut into cubes, then add to theslow cooker.

3. To the cooker, add the apples, stock, salt, pepper, nutmeg, pepper, and cayenne pepper. Cook on low until the apples and squash are tender, about 6-8 hours..

4. Then add the coconut milk. In batches, spoon the contents from the slow cooker into a blender and puree. Transferring the pureed soup back to the slow cooker once done. Now sample the soup and make any adjustments to the seasoning you want. Serve hot with any of your preferred garnishes.

Nutritional Facts:

Calories: 155
Proteins: 3g
Carbs: 31g
Fats: 3g

LENTIL SOUP

Servings: 6

INGREDIENTS

- 2 tbsps. olive oil, extra-virgin
- 1 onion, diced
- 4 carrots, peeled, diced
- 3 stalks celery, chopped fine
- 1½ tsps. Italian seasoning
- 1 tsp. salt
- 1 tsp. smoked paprika
- ½ tsp. pepper
- 4 cloves garlic, minced
- 1/2 cups green lentils
- 1 can fire-roasted tomatoes
- 1 can crushed tomatoes
- 946ml vegetable stock
- Parmesan rind
- 1 tbsp. vinegar, red wine
- ½ tsp. granulated sugar

DIRECTIONS

1. In a skillet,over medium heat warm the olive oil. When hot, add the onion. Cook the onion until tender. Then add in the carrots, celery, Italian seasoning, salt, smoked paprika, and pepper. Sauté until vegetables are slightly tender. Toss in the garlic and cook until fragrant. Transfer mixture to slow cooker.

2. To the cooker, add the lentils, tomatoes, parmesan rind, and vegetable stock. Cook on high low for 6 to 8 hours until the lentils are al dente.

3. Remove the Parmesan rind. Then mix in the vinegar and sugar. Taste and adjust seasoning to taste. Serve hot with a sprinkle of parsley, Parmesan, and crusty bread.

Nutritional Facts:

Calories: 240

Proteins: 12g

Carbs: 36g

Fats: 5g

PEPPER STEAK

Servings: 5

INGREDIENTS

- 907g steak, sliced thin
- 2 tsps. garlic powder
- ½ tsp. salt
- ½ tsp. pepper
- 1 tbsp. grapeseed oil
- 1 onion, sliced
- 59ml cup water
- 2 bell peppers, green, sliced
- 2 bell peppers, red & orange, sliced
- 1 can fire-roasted tomatoes in juices
- 59ml soy sauce
- 2 tbsps. Worcestershire sauce
- 2 tbsps. honey
- 1 tbsp. ginger, fresh, minced
- ¼ tsp. red pepper flakes
- 5 tbsps. cornstarch

DIRECTIONS

1. Place the meat in large bowl and season with garlic powder, salt, and dark pepper. Toss to coat.

2. Heat the grapeseed oil over medium high heat. Then add the meat and cook, browning each side. Move the meat and juices to the slow cooker.

3. Using the same skillet toss in the onions. Raise the heat to high and pour water into the skillet. Scrape up any brown bits and sauté the onions until lightly browned. Move sautéed onions and meat to the cooker. .

4. To the cooker, add the peppers and tomatoes. In a small mixing bowl, whisk together the soy sauce, Worcestershire sauce, honey, ginger, red pepper flakes, and 3 tablespoons cornstarch. Pour mixture into the slow cooker. Cook on low for 6 to 7 hours.

5. Add the remsining cornstarch into water and whisk to make a slurry. Pour the slurry into the cooker and mix well. Turn the Coker up to high and cook for an additional 10 minutes. Taste and adjust seasoning to taste. Serve hot with brown or cauliflower rice and a sprinkle of green onion.

Nutritional Facts:

Calories: 396

Proteins: 42g

Carbs: 29g

Fats: 11g

VEGETABLE BEEF SOUP

Servings: 6

INGREDIENTS

- ♦ 1 tbsp. olive oil, extra virgin
- ♦ 454g stew meat
- ♦ 2 tsps. salt
- ♦ ¼ tsp. pepper
- ♦ 710ml beef broth
- ♦ 1 onion, chopped
- ♦ 2 cloves garlic, minced
- ♦ 4 carrots, peeled, diced fine
- ♦ 2 potatoes, peeled, cubed
- ♦ 2 parsnips, peeled, chopped
- ♦ 2 ribs celery, sliced
- ♦ 1 can tomatoes, diced
- ♦ 1 can tomato puree
- ♦ 3 tbsps. tomato paste
- ♦ 1 tbsp. Worcestershire sauce
- ♦ 1 tsp. dried oregano
- ♦ ½ tsp. smoked paprika
- ♦ ½ tsp. sugar
- ♦ 180g peas, fresh

DIRECTIONS

1. Over medium-high heat in a skillet warm the olive oil. When hot, add the meat and season with 1 tsp. of the salt and pepper. Brown meat and then move to the slow cooker.

2. To the skillet, add the onion. Cook onions until tender then add the garlic and cook for a few seconds more. in the garlic and let cook for30 seconds. In the skillet add some of the stock to deglaze the skillet. Let the stock simmer and reduce and then move to the slow cooker.

3. Then to the stock add in the potatoes, carrots, diced tomatoes in juices, Worcestershire, parsnips, , paprika, pureed tomatoes, celery, tomato paste, oregano, sugar, extra stock, and salt.

4. Turn the cooker to low and let cook for about 8 hours. Mix in the peas, cook until warmed through. Serve hot, sprinkled with freshchopped parsley.

Nutritional Facts:

Calories: 283

Proteins: 24g

Carbs: 33g

Fats: 7g

LETTUCE WRAPS

Servings: 8

INGREDIENTS

- 118ml hoisin sauce
- 59ml soy sauce
- 2 tbsps. rice vinegar
- 2 tsps. sesame oil
- 1 tbsp. olive oil, extra-virgin
- 907g ground chicken
- 1 bundle scallions, finely diced
- 1 tbsp. ginger, fresh, grated
- 2 cloves garlic, minced
- 227g baby mushrooms, chopped fine
- 3 lrg. carrots, shredded
- ½ tsp. red pepper flakes
- 2 cans water chestnuts, drained, chopped fine
- 2 heads butter/bibb lettuce

DIRECTIONS

1. Lightly coat a slow cooker with non-stick spray. In a small bowl, mix together the rice vinegar, hoisin, sesame oil, and soy sauce, Set aside.

2. In a skillet over medium high heat warm some olive oil. When hot, place the chicke in the skillet and brown on all sides. Mix in the ginger, scallions, and garlic. Cook until fragrant.

3. Transfer meat to the slow cooker. Then add the mushrooms, carrots, red pepper flakes, and sauce. Cook on low for 2 -3 hours until thickened. At this point you can add the water chestnuts and more green onions.

4. To serve, separate the spread lettuce leaves and spoon chicken mixture into the cups.

Nutritional Facts:

Calories: 247

Proteins: 28g

Carbs: 21g

Fats: 5g

ITALIAN WEDDING SOUP

Servings: 6

INGREDIENTS

Meatballs:

- 454g ground turkey
- 61g spinach cleaved
- 3 tbsps. coconut flour
- 1 egg
- 2 tbsps. parsley, fresh
- 2 tbsps. basil, fresh
- ¼ tsp. pepper
- 1 tbsp. olive oil
- 1 tsp. garlic, minced

Soup:

- 1 tbsp. olive oil
- ½ tbsp. garlic, minced
- 113g onion, diced
- 1 celery stalk, chopped
- 2 carrots, sliced
- 1 tbsp. rosemary, fresh, chopped fine
- 2 bay leaves
- ¼ tsp. pepper
- 1/8 tsp. red pepper flakes
- 2L chicken stock
- 454g spinach, fresh, chopped
- 454g zucchini noodles

DIRECTIONS

1. Preheat the stove to 232°C. Add all the ingredients for the meatballs to a mixing bowl . On a lined baking sheet, drop 6mm round meatballs. Bake meatballs until browned should be about 10 minutes.

2. While meatballs are cooking, in a skillet, heat olive oil. Add in the onions, celery, garlic, and carrots.Cook onions untiltender. Then transfer them to the cooker Add in the meatballs, stock, and seasonings.

3. Cook the soup on low for 6-8 hours. When the soup is cooked, add in the spinach. Serve over zucchini noodles.

Nutritional Facts:
Calories: 210
Proteins: 23g
Carbs: 12g
Fats: 8g

DINNER

ASIAN INSPIRED ZUCCHINI LASAGNA

Servings: 8

INGREDIENTS

For the zoodles:

- 4 lrg. zucchini
- 1 tbsp. salt

For the lasagna:

- 2 tbsps. coconut oil
- 454g ground turkey
- 171g onion, diced
- 1 tbsp. garlic, minced
- ½ tbsp. ginger, fresh. minced
- Pepper to taste
- 237ml coconut milk
- 59ml peanut butter
- 59ml soy sauce
- 2 tbsps. coconut sugar
- 1 tbsp. rice vinegar
- 1 tbsp. lime juice, fresh
- 1 tbsp. fish sauce
- 2 tbsps. Sriracha
- 425g ricotta
- 1 lrg. egg
- 53g cilantro, fresh, chopped
- 167g cabbage, chopped
- 91g water chestnuts, diced
- 227g mozzarella, shredded
- 1 bell pepper, red, diced

DIRECTIONS

1. Heat the oven to 230°C. Cut the zuccounchini into thin slices (about 1cm) using a mandolin. Spread them out on baking sheets and sprinkle with salt. Let them bake for about twenty minutes to remove water. Slices should be a light brown around the edges.

2. While the zoodles cook, in a skillet heat the oil. Then add in the turkey, onion, garlic, ginger, and a touch of pepper. Cook until the onion is tender, and the turkey is browned (break up the turkey as it cooks).

3. When cooked, include coconut milk, peanut butter, soy sauce, coconut sugar, rice vinegar, lime juice, fish sauce, and the Sriracha. Heat to the point of boiling and simmer for 3 minutes and mix consistently. Turn the heat down and let simmer until the sauce is smooth and has thickened to your desired consistency. Set to the side.

4. Once the zoodles are cooked, move them to a long bit of paper towel, cover with another paper towel, and gently press out as much of the excess water as possible. Repeat until you have removed as much of the water as possible. Set the zoodles aside.

5. In a bowl, use a fork to combine the ricotta, egg, and pepper. Set the mixture aside.

6. Spray the slow cooker with cooking spray. In an even layer, place half of the turkey mixture in the bottom. Then add a layer of the zoodles and then the ricotta mixture. Sprinkle a little cilantro and then some of the cabbage over that. Top with water chestnuts and mozzarella. Repeat this process until the slow cooker is full, and the ingredients are gone. Then top with red peppers and the last bit of mozzarella.

7. Turn the cooker on to low and cook covered for 4-5 hours. Then serve topped with extra cheese and cilantro drizzled with Sriracha.

Nutritional Facts:
Calories: 341
Proteins: 31.2g
Carbs: 15.5g
Fats: 17.1g

ENCHILADA CASSEROLE

Servings: 6

INGREDIENTS

- 680g boneless, skinless chicken bosom
- 1 can pinto beans, drained, rinsed
- 356g quick-cook brown rice
- 1 bell pepper, green, chopped
- 1 bell pepper, yellow, chopped
- ½ onion, diced
- 1 tbsp. minced garlic
- 710ml enchilada sauce
- ½ tbsp. apple juice vinegar
- salt to taste
- 237ml water

DIRECTIONS

1. Add everything into the slow cooker. Mix well and ensure chicken and rice are coated with the wet mixture.

2. Now turn the slow cooker on to low and cook with the lid on for 6-8 hours. After the chocken iscooked, remove and cut into little pieces. Transfer back to the cooker and mix well. Return the lid to the cooker and cook for a couple of additional minutes.

3. Serve topped with yogurt, avocado, cheddar, or any of your favorite toppings.

Nutritional Facts:
Calories: 347
Proteins: 33g
Carbs: 48g
Fats: 5g

LAMB TAGINE

Servings: 4

INGREDIENTS

- 1kg lamb shanks
- 2 lrg. pears, chopped fine
- 534g shallots, diced fine
- 118ml orange juice, fresh
- 118ml pomegranate juice
- 1 tbsp. honey
- 1½ tsps. cinnamon, ground
- 1 tsp. salt
- 1 tsp. ground allspice
- 1 tsp. ground cardamom
- 37g pomegranate seeds
- 27g parsley, fresh, chopped

DIRECTIONS

1. Place lamb into a slow cooker. Add the pears and shallots. In a mixing bowl, combine 59ml orange juice, 59ml pomegranate juice, honey, and seasonings. Mix well and then pour over shallots.

2. Cook, covered, on low for 6-8 hours. Remove shanks and keep warm. Add in the remaining juices with the cooking fluid and then pour over the lamb. Serve garnished with pomegranate seeds and parsley with couscous.

Nutritional Facts:
Calories: 438
Proteins: 31g
Carbs: 52g
Fats: 13g

POACHED SALMON

Servings: 8

INGREDIENTS

- 1.5L water
- 1 onion, diced
- 2 stalks of celery, chopped
- 4 sprigs parsley, fresh
- 118ml white wine
- 1 tbsp. soy sauce
- 8 peppercorns
- 1 bay leaf
- 1 salmon filet
- 1 lemon, cut into wedges
- Dill, fresh, chopped

DIRECTIONS

1. In a large pan, combine everything but the lemon, dill, and salmon. Let simmer for half an hour. Then strain the mixture.

2. Cut three pieces of foil and place them in the cooker like a tire spoke pour the poaching fluid into the base. Set the fish gently into insert. .

3. Set the cooker;s temperature to high and cook with the lid on for about an hour. Use the foil as handles, remove the salmon from cooking fluid. Garnish with dill and lemon wedges and serve either cold or hot.

Nutritional Facts:
Calories: 266
Proteins: 29g
Carbs: 0g
Fats: 16g

BEEF BARBACOA

Servings: 8

INGREDIENTS

- 1 beef rump roast
- 53g cilantro, fresh, chopped
- 78ml tomato paste
- 8 garlic cloves, minced
- 2 tbsps. chipotle peppers in adobo sauce
- 2 tbsps. apple cider vinegar
- 4 tsps. cumin, ground
- 1 tbsp. brown sugar
- 1½ tsps. salt
- 1 tsp. pepper
- 237ml beef stock
- 237ml lager
- 16 sm. corn tortillas
- Salsa

DIRECTIONS

1. Cut roast into smaller pieces. Combine the cilantro, tomato paste, garlic, peppers, vinegar, cumin, sugar, salt, and pepper. Then rub the roast with the spice mixture. Place roast int the cooer and turn it on to low. Let it cook for 6-8 hours.

2. Remove the meat and shred with 2 forks. Save 710ml of the cooking juices. Skim fat from the reserved juices. Return meat and juices to the slow cooker, heat through.

3. Serve on tortillas topped with salsa and other toppings of your taste.

Nutritional Facts:

Calories: 361
Proteins: 38g
Carbs: 28g
Fats: 10g

CHICKEN WINGZ

Servings: 6

INGREDIENTS

- ◆ 1.5kg chicken wings
- ◆ 237ml BBQ Sauce
- ◆ Salt and pepper to taste

DIRECTIONS

1. Defrost chicken wings in the refrigerator and when thawed season with salt and pepper.

2. Lightly coat the slow cooker with cooking spray. Pour in half of the BBQ sauce. And then place chicken in a slow cooker. Toss chicken until coated. Set bcooker to high and cook for about 2 hours.

3. Preheat the oven to 204˚C. Remove chicken from the slow cooker to an oiled baking sheet. Brush on the leftover BBQ sauce Bake chicken wings for 15-20 minutes, turning halfway through the cooking. Serve hot, garnished with chopped scallions with ranch or blue cheese dressing.

Nutritional Facts:
Calories: 365
Proteins: 29g
Carbs: 6g
Fats: 25g

JAMBALAYA

Servings: 12

INGREDIENTS

- 1 can diced tomatoes with juices
- 237ml chicken stock
- 1 bell pepper, green, chopped
- 1 onion, chopped
- 2 celery stalks, chopped
- 118ml white wine
- 4 garlic cloves, minced
- 2 tsps. Cajun preparing
- 2 tsps. parsley, dried
- 1 tsp. basil, dried
- 1 tsp. oregano, dried
- ¾ tsp. salt
- ½ tsp. cayenne pepper
- 907g chicken thighs,boneless, skinless, cut into cubes
- 1 pkg. chicken sausage
- 2 pounds shrimp, peeled and deveined

DIRECTIONS

1. Add all the ingredienst excluding te meats and shrimp into a bowl. Mix well. Place chicken and chicken sausage into the cooker and then add the liquid over the top. Cook, covered, on low until chicken is delicate, 7-9 hours.

2. At the very end add in the shrimp and cook for an additional 15-20 minutes longer. Serve over brown rice and garnished with scallions.

Nutritional Facts:

Calories: 387

Proteins: 36g

Carbs: 37g

Fats: 10g

SOUTHWESTERN CASSEROLE

Servings: 8

INGREDIENTS

- 1 onion, diced
- 1 jalapeno, sliced
- 1 tbsp. canola oil
- 2 garlic cloves, minced
- 1 can kidney beans, drained, rinsed
- 1 can pinto beans, drained, rinsed

- 1 can diced tomatoes with juices
- 1 can crushed tomatoes
- 1 tsp. chili powder
- ½ tsp. pepper
- 1/8 tsp. hot sauce

Cornbread:

- 125g all-purpose flour
- 159g yellow cornmeal
- 1 tbsp. sugar
- 1½ tsps. baking powder
- ½ tsp. salt
- 2 lrg. eggs
- 296ml milk
- 1 can creamed corn
- 3 tbsps. canola oil

DIRECTIONS

1. Add the onions and jalepeno to a heated skillet with oil and sautee until softened. Then toss in the garlic and cook until fragrant. Transfer to the slow cooker.

2. Then toss in everything else in the main dish ingredients. Turn the cooker to high and cook covered for about an hour.

3. Add the dry ingredinest for the cornbread toa large mixing bowl. Mix to combine. In a separate bowl do te same for the wet ingredients. Then begin to add in the dry to the wet. Mix until combined thoroughly. Spoon evenly over bean blend.

4. Return the lid to the cooker and cook for an additional 2- 3 hours,a toothpick should be able to be inserted and removed clean. Tp with y9r favorite garnishes and enjoy.

Nutritional Facts:
Calories: 367
Proteins: 14g
Carbs: 59g
Fats: 9g

CHICKEN TIKKA MASALA

Servings: 6

INGREDIENTS

- 680g. chicken breast, boneless, skinless
- 2 potatoes, cubed
- 1 onion, diced
- 1 can coconut milk
- 1 can tomato sauce
- 2 tbsps. garam masala
- 1 tsp. ground cumin
- ½ tsp. ground turmeric
- ½ tsp. garlic powder
- 1/8 tsp. ground ginger
- 1/8 tsp. salt

DIRECTIONS

1. Pour coconut milk, tomatoes, and seasonings into the slow cooker and mix. Then add the potatoes and onion and stir. Now place the chicken on top and make sure sauce is surrounding it. Cover and cook on low for 6-8 hours.

2. When the chicken is completely cooked, remove and cut into pieces. Then transfer chocken back to the cooker and mix to combine Serve over rice.

Nutritional Facts:
Calories: 315
Proteins: 24g
Carbs: 10g
Fats: 14g

GREEN CHILE BEEF

Servings: 12

INGREDIENTS

- 2 onions, diced fine
- 4 tbsps. brown sugar
- 1 tbsp. paprika
- 1½ tsps. salt
- 1 tsp. cayenne pepper
- 1 tsp. chili powder
- 1 tsp. garlic powder
- ½ tsp. pepper
- 1 boneless roast
- 2 tbsps. canola oil
- 1 can green chili sauce

DIRECTIONS

1. Place onions and 3 tablespoons brown sugar in the slow cooker. Mix the rest of the brown sugar with the reaming herbs and seaosnings. Combine and rub on roast.

2. Over medium high heat warm the canola oil and brown roast on each side. Then transfer to a slow cooker and pour green chili sauce over the top. Cook on low for 7-9 hours. Remove roast and shred. Return shredded meat to the cooker and heat for a few more minutes. Serve hot over mashed potatoes.

Nutritional Facts:
Calories: 278
Proteins: 23g
Carbs: 14g
Fats: 15g

APPLE BUTTER GLAZED PORK W/ WHITE BEANS

Servings: 10

INGREDIENTS

- 12 ounces baby carrots, chopped
- 1 onion, diced
- 1 pork loin
- 1½ tsps. salt
- ½ tsp. pepper
- 1 tbsp. olive oil
- 237ml apple butter
- 2 tbsps. apple cider vinegar
- 1 tbsp. Dijon mustard
- 3 garlic cloves, minced
- 2 jars cannellini beans, drained, rinsed

DIRECTIONS

1. Place carrots and onion in the slow cooker. Sprinkle loin with a tsp. of salt and 1/4 tsp. of pepper. Heat olive oil over medium high heat and brown the loin. Then move to a slow cooker.

2. Combine the apple butter, salt, vinegar, pepper, mustard, and garlic in a bowl and mix well. , Add this over the top of the loin and vegetables. Cook on low for 3-1/2 to 4-1/2 hours.

3. Remove loin and keep warm. Add the beans and let cook for another half hour. Serve sliced pork loin over the bean mixture.

Nutritional Facts:

Calories: 314
Proteins: 31g
Carbs: 28g
Fats: 8g

TURKEY CHILI

Servings: 6

INGREDIENTS

- 454g ground turkey
- 1 onion, chopped
- 2 cups chicken broth
- 1 can pumpkin puree
- 1 can green chiles
- 1 tbsp. chili powder
- 1 tsp. garlic powder
- 1 tsp. ground cumin
- 1 tsp. curry powder
- ½ tsp. dried oregano
- ½ tsp. salt
- 1 can cannellini beans, rinsed, drained

DIRECTIONS

1. In a skillet, cook the turkey and onion over medium heat until the turkey is browned, and onion is tender, making sure to break up the turkey as you go. Then transfer to the slow cooker.

2. Add in the stock, pumpkin puree, chiles, and seasonings. Cook on low for 4-5 hours. Then toss in the beans; cook until warmed through, around 60 minutes.

3. Serve over rice or garnished with your favorite toppings.

Nutritional Facts:

Calories: 243
Proteins: 20g
Carbs: 27g
Fats: 6g

CANTONESE PORK LOIN

Servings: 10

INGREDIENTS

- 3 tbsps. honey
- 2 tbsps. soy sauce
- 1 tbsp. sesame oil
- 1 tbsp. mirin
- 4 garlic cloves, minced
- 1 tsp. ginger, fresh, minced
- 1 tsp. hoisin sauce
- 1 tsp. fish sauce
- 1 tsp. Chinese five-spice
- 1 tsp. salt
- 1 tsp. red food coloring
- 1 boneless pork loin

DIRECTIONS

1. In a bowl, add everything but the food coloring and pork and mix well. Then add in the coloring and mix again. Cut loin down the center and add to the bowl. Cover the bowl and refrigerate overnight.

2. Add pork along with juices it marinaded in to the cooker Cook on low 3-4 hours. Once done, let pork rest for about 15 minutes. Slice and serve on abed of your chosen grain.

Nutritional Facts:
Calories: 263
Proteins: 36g
Carbs: 6g
Fats: 10g

CHICKEN CACCIATORE

Servings: 4

INGREDIENTS

- 1 bell pepper, red, diced
- 1 bell pepper, green, diced
- 5 cloves garlic, minced
- 680g. chicken breast. boneless, skinless
- ½ onion, diced
- 1 can black olives, sliced, drained
- 1 can tomato sauce
- 1 can diced tomatoes
- 2 tbsps. balsamic vinegar
- 1 tbsp. Italian seasoning
- salt to taste
- 6 sprigs thyme, fresh
- 6 sprigs rosemary. fresh
- 227g pasta of choice

DIRECTIONS

1. Place peppers, garlic, chicken, onion, and olives into the slow cooker.

2. In a mixing bowl, combine tomato sauce, diced tomatoes, balsamic vinegar, Italian seasoning, and salt. Combine and add into the slow cooker. Then tie the thyme and rosemary with twine and place in the cooker as well.

3. Cover and cook on low for 6-8 hours. When the chicken has completely cooked, remove, and shred. Remove the herbs parcel and replace chicken into the cooker. Let cook for an additional couple fo minutes.

4. Serve over pasta topped with Parmesan.

Nutritional Facts:

Calories: 471
Proteins: 35g
Carbs: 63g
Fats: 6g

MUSHROOM MARSALA

Servings: 6

INGREDIENTS

- 680g baby mushrooms, chopped
- 147g shallots, diced fine
- 3 tbsps. olive oil
- ½ tsp. thyme, fresh, minced
- 177ml Marsala wine
- 3 tbsps. sour cream
- 2 tbsps. all-purpose flour
- 1½ tsps. lemon zest, fresh
- ¼ tsp. salt
- 43g feta, crumbled
- 27g parsley, fresh, chopped

DIRECTIONS

1. Combine the mushrooms, shallots, olive oil, and thyme in the slow cooker. Include 59ml of Marsala wine. Cook on low for around 4 hours.

2. Mix in the sour cream, flour, lemon zest, salt and rest of the Marsala. Cook on low 15 minutes longer. Top with feta and parsley and serve over a grain of your choice.

Nutritional Facts:

Calories: 235
Proteins: 7g
Carbs: 31g
Fats: 9g

PICADILLO

Servings: 6

INGREDIENTS

- ½ tbsp. olive oil
- 907g ground beef
- ½ onion, minced
- 1 tbsp. garlic, minced
- 2 tbsps. jalapeno, minced
- 1 can crushed tomatoes
- 1 cup bone broth
- 1 tsp. cinnamon
- 1 tsp. pepper
- 1 tsp. garlic powder
- 1 tsp. salt
- 1 tsp. chili powder
- 2 tsps. cumin
- 1 tsp. paprika
- 113g raisins
- 57g green olives

DIRECTIONS

1. Over medium heat warm olive oil. Then add in the meat and cook until browned. Then transfer to the slow cooker.. Add in everything else and stir to combine.

2. Cook on low for 8 hours. Serve over cauliflower rice topped with garnishes of your choice.

Nutritional Facts:

Calories: 360
Proteins: 33g
Carbs: 18g
Fats: 18g

BALSAMIC PORK ROAST

Servings: 8

INGREDIENTS

- 907g boneless pork shoulder
- Salt to taste
- ½ tsp. garlic powder
- ½ tsp. red pepper flakes
- 78ml vegetable stock
- 78ml balsamic vinegar
- 1 tbsp. Worcestershire sauce
- 1 tbsp. honey

DIRECTIONS

1. Season the pork with garlic powder, red pepper flakes, and salt and add to theslow cooker.

2. Combine the stock, vinegar, and Worcestershire saucein a bowl and pour it over the pork. Pour the honey over the pork and cook for 6-8 hours on low.

3. When the pork is cooked and delicate, remove from the cooker and place on serving dish.

4. Shred gently with two forks and transfer meat back into the slow cooker. Scoop 118ml sauce over the pork and keep warm until prepared to eat. Serve with noodles or mashed cauliflower.

Nutritional Facts:

Calories: 214

Proteins: 21g

Carbs: 4g

Fats: 12g

CHICKEN FAJITAS

Servings: 10

INGREDIENTS

- 1kg chicken breast, boneless, skinless
- 1 can diced tomatoes
- 1 can green chiles, diced
- 2 tbsps. taco seasoning
- 3 bell peppers, sliced
- 1 lime, juiced

DIRECTIONS

1. Add tomatoes and chiles into the slow cooker. Place chicken on top and season with taco preparation. Turn cooker onto high and cook covered for 3 hours.

2. Then add the peppers and cover. Let cook for 1 more hour.

3. Remove the chicken from the cooker and shred with a fork. Return the shredded chicken back to the cooker. Now toss in the lime juice and stir to combine. Adjust seasoning and serve on whole wheat tortillas topped with your favorite garnishes.

Nutritional Facts:

Calories: 140

Proteins: 23g

Carbs: 6g

Fats: 3g

BONUS

VEGETARIAN

EGGPLANT PARMESAN

Servings: 12

INGREDIENTS

- 2kg eggplant
- 1 tbsp. salt
- 3 lrg. eggs
- 59ml milk
- 53g breadcrumbs
- 85g Parmesan
- 2 tsps. Italian seasoning
- 946ml marinara sauce
- 453g mozzarella, shredded
- Basil, fresh, chopped

DIRECTIONS

1. Peeland cut the eggplant into .84cm slices. Lay the slices in a colander and salt. Allow the eggplabt to sit for half an hour and then pat dry. Coat bottom of slow cooker with 118ml of marinara.

2. Whisk together the eggs and milk in a bowl. Mix together breadcrumbs, Parmesan, and Italian seasoning in a different bowl. Dunk eggplant in egg blend and then the breadcrumbs.

3. Layer 1/3 of the eggplant into the slow cooker. Top the layer with another 236ml of marinara and some of the mozzarella. Repeat the process for the remaining layers.. Top with remaining mozzarella and cook on low for eight hours.

4. Serve topped with fresh basil and extra Parmesan.

Nutritional Facts:
Calories: 258
Proteins: 16g
Carbs: 23g
Fats: 12g

VEGETABLE POT PIE

Servings: 6

INGREDIENTS

- 1273g various chopped vegetables (mushrooms, Brussel sprouts, carrots, peas, and potatoes)
- ½ onion, diced
- 4 cloves garlic, minced
- 5 sprigs thyme, fresh, leaves separated
- 31g flour
- 473ml cups chicken stock
- 41g cornstarch
- 59ml heavy cream
- salt and pepper to taste
- 1 sheet puff pastry, defrosted
- 2 tbsps. butter

DIRECTIONS

1. Clean and prepare the vegetables and with the garlic and onion place in the cooker. Toss in the four and coat the vegetables. Slowly mix in the stock until flour is thoroughly combined with it. Cover and cook on low for 6-8.

2. Whisk cornstarch with water to create a slurry then pour into vegetable mix. Add the cream as well as the butter, then raise the temp to high and cook for another 15 minutes until thickened.

3. Preheat the oven to 204°C. On a baking sheet place puff pastry Melt 2 tablespoons of butter and brush the top of the pastry with it. Then bake for 10 minutes or until puffed and lightly brown. Serve the vegetable mixture topped with a portion of puff pastry.

Nutritional Facts:
Calories: 489
Proteins: 12g
Carbs: 59g
Fats: 24g

LENTIL BOLOGNESE

Servings: 6

INGREDIENTS

- 2 tbsps. olive oil
- ½ onion, diced
- 2 carrots, shredded
- 3 celery stalks, diced
- 4 garlic cloves, minced
- ½ tsp. red pepper flakes
- 227g dried lentils, rinsed
- 1 can crushed tomatoes
- 710ml vegetable stock
- 1 bay leaf
- 1 tbsps. dried basil
- ½ tbsp. dried parsley
- 1 tsp. salt

DIRECTIONS

1. Place everything into the slow cooker. Stir until combined thoroughly. Cook on low for 4 – 5 hours, or until lentils have become slightly tender and sauce is thick.

2. Adjust seasoning to taste. Serve over whole-wheat pasta.

Nutritional Facts:
Calories: 250
Proteins: 12.3g
Carbs: 41.4g
Fats: 5.6g

CHILI MAC

Servings: 6

INGREDIENTS

- 1 onion, chopped
- 1 bell pepper, red, chopped
- 1 can pinto beans, rinsed, drained
- 1 can kidney beans, rinsed, drained
- 1 can crushed tomatoes
- 1½ tbsps. chili powder
- 2 tsps. cumin
- ½ tsp. salt
- 1/8 tsp. pepper
- 473ml vegetable stock
- 227g whole wheat macaroni, uncooked
- 1½ cups cheddar, shredded
- Scallions, chopped

DIRECTIONS

1. Place all the ingredients in the slow cooker except the cheese and scallions. Turn the cooker on to low and let cook for about 4-6 hours until pasta is al dente. Then serve topped with your favorite garnishes.

Nutritional Facts:
Calories: 428
Proteins: 22g
Carbs: 64g
Fats: 16g

QUINOA TACOS

Servings: 6

INGREDIENTS

- ♦ 159g quinoa
- ♦ 237ml vegetable stock
- ♦ 2 cans black beans
- ♦ 1 can diced tomatoesin tomato juice
- ♦ 1 can enchilada sauce
- ♦ 1 can corn
- ♦ 3 tbsps. taco seasoning
- ♦ Corn or flour tortillas

DIRECTIONS

1. Rinse quinoa in a fine-mesh colander. Then add to the slow cooker everything else (excluding the tortillas). Mix ingredients together. Cover and cook on high 2.5 hours to 4 hours.

2. When quinoa is cooked through, serve on tortillas and top with your ideal garnishes.

Nutritional Facts:

Calories: 136

Proteins: 5.2g

Carbs: 22.6g

Fats: 3g

PINEAPPLE CURRY

Servings: 4

INGREDIENTS

- 1 can coconut milk
- 3 tbsps. curry powder
- 1½ tsps. salt
- 1 tsp.red pepper flakes
- 1½ tsp. garlic powder
- 1 pineapple, fresh, cut into pieces
- 453g of yams, stripped and cubed
- 2 bell peppers, green, chopped
- 2 onions, chopped
- 2 cans garbanzo beans, rinsed, drained

DIRECTIONS

1. Whisk together the garlic, coconut milk, red pepper flakes, curry powder, and salt , and in the slow cooker.

2. Then add in everything else and stir until mixed. Cover and cook on low for 6-8 hours oruntil yams are tender but not mushy.

Nutritional Facts:
Calories: 252
Proteins: 5.7g
Carbs: 59g
Fats: 1.2g

BUTTERNUT SQUASH DAL

Servings: 6

INGREDIENTS

- 1 tbsp.olive oil
- 2 onions. chopped
- 4 cloves garlic, minced
- 1 butternut squash, ubed
- 113g dry lentils, red
- 400ml coconut milk
- 796ml diced tomatoes
- 1 tbsp. turmeric
- 1 tbsp. curry powder
- 1 tsp. chili powder
- 1 tsp. salt
- ¼ tsp. pepper
- 150g spinach, chopped

Basmati rice

- 178g basmati rice
- 59ml water
- 1 tsp. spread
- Pinch of salt

DIRECTIONS

1. Add everything excluding the rice and the spinach) to the slow cooker. Cook on low for 8 hours.

2. Then, prepare the rice per the instructions. When dal is done cooking, mix in spinach and serve with rice.

Nutritional Facts:

Calories: 383
Proteins: 16g
Carbs: 72g
Fats: 4g

RATATOUILLE

Servings: 8

INGREDIENTS

- 2 tbsps. coconut oil
- 1 onion, diced
- 6 cloves garlic, minced
- 1 eggplant, sliced
- 1 bell pepper, orange, chopped
- 4 zucchini
- 150g grape tomatoes, quartered
- 2 tbsps. tomato paste
- 1 tsp. oregano, dried
- 1 tsp. pepper
- 1 tsp. salt
- ¼ tsp. red pepper flakes
- 83g basil, fresh, chopped

DIRECTIONS

1. Throw everything excluding the basil into the slow cooker. Mix well. Cover and cook 5-6 hours on low.

2. Serve warm or cold as a side or over the grain of your choice.

Nutritional Facts:

Calories: 127

Proteins: 5g

Carbs: 23g

Fats: 5g

SPAGHETTI SQUASH

Servings: 4

INGREDIENTS

- 1 spaghetti squash
- 1 can diced tomatoes with juices
- 150g mushrooms, fresh, chopped
- ½ tsp. salt
- ½ tsp. dried oregano
- ¼ tsp. pepper
- 63g mozzarella, shredded

DIRECTIONS

1. Cut squash in half and clean out the seeds. Load up with tomatoes and mushrooms, and sprinkle with seasonings. Place in a slow cooker.

2. Cook on low until squash is delicate, 6-8 hours. Sprinkle with cheddar. Return the lid and cook until the cheese is melted, about 10 minutes more. Serve topped with additional cheese or garnished with basil.

Nutritional Facts:

Calories: 195
Proteins: 9g
Carbs: 31g
Fats: 6g

TORTILLA LASAGNA

Servings: 8

INGREDIENTS

- 1 can diced tomatoes with basil, oregano, and garlic
- 237ml thick salsa
- 1 can tomato paste
- ½ tsp. ground cumin
- 2 cans hominy, rinsed, drained
- 1 can black beans, rinsed, drained
- 3 flour tortillas (10 inches)
- 167g Monterey Jack cheese, shredded
- 16g black olives, sliced

DIRECTIONS

1. Tear off three pieces of foil and place them in the slow cooker so that they cross each other.. Spray the foil lightly with nonsticj cooking spray.

2. In a huge bowl, combine the tomatoes, salsa, tomato paste, and cumin. Then add in the beans and hominy. Place one tortilla on the bottom of the slow cooker. Top it with a third of the mixture. Then repeat for the next two layers. Top with olives. Turn slow cooker to low and cook for approximately 3 to 3-1/2 hours or until warmed through.

3. Use foil as handles and move the lasagna to a platter. Let it cool and then you can slice it into portions. Serve topped with your favorite toppings.

Nutritional Facts:
Calories: 355
Proteins: 15g
Carbs: 41g
Fats: 12g

VEGAN

LENTIL & CAULIFLOWER CURRY

Servings: 8

INGREDIENTS

- 294g dried lentils, red
- 1 onion, chopped
- 2 cloves garlic, minced
- 1 head cauliflower, chopped
- 1 tbsp. ginger, fresh, minced
- 2 tbsps. curry paste, red
- ½ tsp. salt
- 1 tsp. ground turmeric
- ½ tsp. ground coriander
- ½ tsp. ground cumin
- ½ tsp. cayenne pepper
- ¼ tsp. ground cardamom
- 1 can tomato puree
- 118ml coconut milk
- Cilantro, fresh, chopped
- Brown rice

DIRECTIONS

1. Place the lentils and cauliflower in the slow cooker. Then add in the onions, garlic, cauliflower, ginger, curry paste, salt, turmeric, coriander, cumin, cayenne, and cardamom. Mix ingredients together.

2. Pour the tomato puree over the head of the cauliflower and lentils. Then fill the can with water and add that as well. Set cooker to low and cook covered for about 7-8 hours, until the lentils are tender but not mushy.

3. Before serving, add in the coconut milk, mix well and let warm through. Serve over brown rice garnished with fresh cilantro.

Nutritional Facts:
Calories: 232
Proteins: 14.4g
Carbs: 43g
Fats: 2g

SAAG PANEER VEGAN STYLE

Servings: 6

INGREDIENTS

- 2 tbsps. olive oil
- 1 onion, diced
- 5 cloves garlic, minced
- 3 tbsps. ginger, fresh, grated
- 2 tbsps. garam masala
- 1 tbsp. coriander, ground
- 1 tbsp. turmeric
- 1 tbsp. cumin, ground
- 1 tsp. cayenne pepper
- 1 tsp. mustard seeds
- 1 chili, diced fine
- 907g frozen spinach, defrosted, pressed
- 1 can coconut milk
- 237mlpureed tomatoes
- 1 tsp. salt
- 1 pkg. extra-firm tofu, drained, squeezed
- 2 tsps. cornstarch
- Basmati rice and naan, for serving

DIRECTIONS

1. In a skillet heat some of the olive oil. Toss in the onions when oil is warmed and cook until translucent

2. Then toss in the garlic, ginger, seasonings, and chili and cook until brown nd fragrant. Take this mixture and scrape it into a food processor. In batches, pulse the spinach with the seasoning blend.

3. When done, place in the slow cooker and add in the coconut milk, pureed tomatoes, and salt. Cook on low for 6 hours.

4. Half an hour before serving, dice up the tofu and toss with corn starch. Warm some oil in a skillet and add the tofu. Brown on all sides and then add the tofu to the spinach mix. Gently stir and let heat through for a few minutes. Serve warm over rice with naan.

Nutritional Facts:

Calories: 290
Proteins: 12g
Carbs: 36g
Fats: 11g

VEGETABLE LO MEIN

Servings: 4

INGREDIENTS

- ◆ 118ml vegetable stock
- ◆ 3 tbsps. hoisin sauce
- ◆ 2 tbsps. soy sauce
- ◆ 2 tsps. honey
- ◆ 1 tsp. soy sauce, light
- ◆ 1 tsp. sesame oil
- ◆ ½ tbsp. mirin
- ◆ ½ tsp. red chili flakes
- ◆ 2 garlic cloves, minced
- ◆ ½ tbsp. ginger, fresh, minced
- ◆ 1 pkg. extra firm tofu
- ◆ 89g carrots, julienned
- ◆ 1 bell pepper, red, chopped fine
- ◆ 171g snow peas, sliced
- ◆ 32g frozen edamame
- ◆ ½ pkg. Lo Mein noodles
- ◆ 2 tbsps. cornstarch
- ◆ sesame seeds

DIRECTIONS

1. Lightly spray the slow cooker with a non-stick cooking spray. Cobine all the ingredinets for the sauce in the cooker and whisk them together. Then add the garlic and ginger . Mix well then place tofu block into the sauce. Cook on low for 1-2 hours, flipping the tofu over part of the way through.

2. While that is cooking, prepare the noodles per the package instructions. Set aside.

3. Remove tofu and cut into pieces to Then return the tofu to the slow cooker. Raise the temperature to high and cook for another hour.

4. Then 30 minutes before serving, toss in the noodles. To thicken the sauce, whisk together cornstarch and water in a little bowl and mix into the cooker. Cover and let cook until the sauce thickens up Then toss again so that everything is nicely coated.

5. Serve garnished with chopped scallions and toasted sesame seeds.

Nutritional Facts:

Calories: 528

Proteins: 15g

Carbs: 106g

Fats: 4g

KUNG PAO CHICKPEAS

Servings: 6

INGREDIENTS

- ½ onion, chopped
- 1 bell pepper, red, diced
- 2 cans chickpeas, rinsed, drained
- 59ml tamari
- 2 tbsps. balsamic vinegar
- 2 tbsps. maple syrup
- ½ tsp. garlic powder
- ½ tsp. ground ginger
- 1 tsp. red pepper flakes
- 1 tsp. toasted sesame oil
- 3 scallions, sliced
- sesame seeds
- Steamed rice

DIRECTIONS

1. Add the onion, bell pepper, and chickpeas into the slow cooker. In a bowl, whisk together the tamari, vinegar, maple syrup, garlic, ginger, red pepper flakes, and sesame oil. Mix well and then add not a slow cooker.

2. Cover the cooker and cook for 6 hours on low. When the cooking is done, stir the chickpeas and serve them over the grain of your choicewith a sprinkling of scallions and sesame seeds.

Nutritional Facts:
Calories: 120
Proteins: 5g
Carbs: 19g
Fats: 2g

ORZO SOUP

Servings: 6

INGREDIENTS

- 178g orzo
- 473ml water
- 473ml vegetable stock
- 2 tbsps. vegan butter
- 2 tbsps. garlic, minced
- 43g onion, finely diced
- 171g corn
- 167g spinach, chopped
- 2 tbsps. basil, dried
- 1 tbsp. salt
- 1 tbsp. pepper

DIRECTIONS

1. Place all the ingredients into the slow cooker except the vegetable stock.

2. Turn the cooker on high and cover the orzo with the water. Cook for about two hours or until the orzo is al dente.

3. Then turn the cooker onto the warm setting and add the vegetable stock. Mix the soup together. Serve with bread and vegan Parmesan.

Nutritional Facts:

Calories: 236
Proteins: 5g
Carbs: 29g
Fats: 78g

VEGAN MEATLOAF

Servings: 6

INGREDIENTS

Veggie Loaf

- 1 can kidney beans, drained (save 60 mL of the fluid)
- 110g rolled oats, ground into flour
- 55g walnuts
- 1 portobello mushroom, cleaned, minced
- 2 tbsps. nutritional yeast
- 2 tbsps. tomato paste

- 1 tbsp. vegan Worcestershire sauce
- 1 tsp. onion powder
- 1 tsp. salt
- 1 tsp. thyme
- 1 tsp. marjoram
- ½ tsp. smoked paprika
- ½ tsp. garlic powder
- ¼ tsp. ground rosemary

Topping

- 120g ketchup
- 3 tbsps. brown sugar
- 1 tbsp. balsamic vinegar
- 1 tbsp. vegan Worcestershire sauce

DIRECTIONS

1. Mix all the loaf ingredients together the night before and refrigerate them in a covered container. Also, mix the topping sauce and refrigerate it as well.

2. Lightly spray the slow cooker the next day and line with parchment paper. Shape the loaf mixture into the slow cooker. Cover and cook on low for about 7 -9 hours.

3. About 30 to 45 minutes before serving, pour the topping over the loaf. Let cook for a few more minutes and then serve with mashed cauliflower.

Nutritional Facts:

Calories: 195

Proteins: 10g

Carbs: 28g

Fats: 10g

FAUX BUFFALO CHICKEN SANDWICHES

Servings: 4

INGREDIENTS

- 1 sm. bottle of hot sauce
- 162g vegan butter
- 1 tsp. garlic powder
- 1 tbsps. vegan Worcestershire
- 2 tbsps. nutritional yeast
- ½ tbsps. dill, dried
- 2 cans jackfruit rinsed, drained
- 4 hamburger buns
- 4 slices of vegancheddar

DIRECTIONS

1. Add the butter, hot sauce, Worcestershire, garlic powder, nutritional yeast, and dill to a slow cooker set on low. Let the ingredients cook stirring every now and then for about 10 minutes.occasionally.

2. Then, once the sauce is heated up, add in the jackfruit and cook for 3 hours. About two hours in, remove the jackfruit and shred with 2 forks and keep cooking. When done, serve on buns topped with cheese and your favorite vegan condiments.

Nutritional Facts:

Calories: 466

Proteins: 11g

Carbs: 8g

Fats: 45g

GARLIC ARTICHOKES

Servings: 6

INGREDIENTS

- ◆ 2 artichokes
- ◆ 473ml vegetable stock
- ◆ 59ml olive oil
- ◆ 2 tbsps. soy sauce
- ◆ 1 tbsp. pepper
- ◆ 2 tbsps. onion powder
- ◆ 3 tbsps. garlic, minced

DIRECTIONS

1. Turn the slow cooker on to high and add the vegetable stock, olive oil, soy sauce, garlic, and seasonings into the slow cooker Whisk mixture until combined.

2. Place the artichokes into the stock, spoon a portion of the stock over the artichokes

3. Cfor 2 hours, covered, or until artichokes are tender.

Nutritional Facts:
Calories: 141
Proteins: 3g
Carbs: 12g
Fats: 10g

RAMEN W/ MUSHROOMS

Servings: 4

INGREDIENTS

- 946ml water
- 28g dried shiitakes
- 1 tbsps. white miso
- 85g onion. minced
- 3 garlic cloves, minced
- 2 tbsps. soy sauce
- 177ml coconut milk
- 2 tbsps. sesame oil
- 1 tbsps. olive oil
- 1 tbsps. vegan Worcestershire sauce
- ½ sheet Kombu
- ½ tbsps. ginger, fresh, minced
- 2 tsps. Mirin
- 1 tsp. salt
- 2 pcs. lemongrass, crushed
- Scallions, chopped
- 2 bundles ramen noodles
- 2 pkgs. maitake mushrooms, sliced

DIRECTIONS

1. Add the water, shiitakes, miso, coconut milk, onion, garlic, 1 tbsp. soy sauce, 2 tbs olive oil, Worcestershire sauce, kombu, ginger, mirin, lemongrass, and salt into the cookernd in the slow cooker. Stir to combine. Set cooker to high and let cook covered for about 2-3 hours.

2. About half an hour before done, warm the olive oil in a skillet. When hot, add in the mushrooms and sprinkle with salt. Cook for 7 minutes flip, sprinkle the other side with a touch of salt, and cook for an additional 5 minutes. Sprinkle with remaining soy sauce and set the mushrooms to the side.

3. Cook ramen noodles as directed When al dente, drain the water. Separate the cooked noodles into different bowls. Then when the stock is cooked, remove the kombu and lemongrass. Then spoon the broth over the noodles and top with the sautéed mushrooms and scallions.

Nutritional Facts:

Calories: 478

Proteins: 13g

Carbs: 47g

Fats: 29g

MAC -N- CHEESE

Servings: 12

INGREDIENTS

- 454g macaroni dry
- 710ml soy milk
- 227g vegan mozzarella
- 680g vegan cheese, shredded
- 57g vegan butter
- 1 tsp. salt
- 3 tbsps. nutritional yeast

DIRECTIONS

1. Set the slow cooker to high and add in all the ingredients except the noodles. Then stir them together until they are combined thoroughly. Stir periodically as the sauce cooks.

2. About 2 hours into cooking, throw in the pasta noodles, and stir into sauce. Cook for another until the noodles are al dente, about 20 minutes.

Nutritional Facts:

Calories: 409

Proteins: 23g

Carbs: 34g

Fats: 20g

Printed by Amazon Italia Logistica S.r.l.
Torrazza Piemonte (TO), Italy

14948811R00064